What Should Know About ... Listening

Judi Brownell
Cornell University

Andrew Wolvin
University of Maryland

Allyn & Bacon
Boston Columbus Indianapolis New York San Francisco Upper Saddle River Amsterdam
Cape Town Dubai London Madrid Milan Munich Paris Montreal Toronto Delhi
Mexico City Sao Paulo Sydney Hong Kong Seoul Singapore Taipei Tokyo

Editor-in-Chief: Karon Bowers
Acquisitions Editor: Jeanne Zalesky
Assistant Editor: Megan Lentz
Marketing Manager: Blair Tuckman
Senior Managing Editor: Linda Mihatov Behrens
Production Editor: Bayani Mendoza de Leon
Editorial Production Service: Pre-Press PMG
Manufacturing Buyer: Mary Ann Gloriande
Electronic Composition: Pre-Press PMG
Cover Administrator/Designer: Anne Bonanno Nieglos

Copyright © 2010 Pearson Education, Inc., Publishing as Allyn & Bacon, 75 Arlington Street, Suite 300, Boston, MA 02116

All Rights Reserved. Manufactured in the United States of America. No part of the material protected by this copyright notice may be reproduced or utilized in any form or by any means, electronic or mechanical, including photocopying, recording, or by any information storage and retrieval system, without written permission from the copyright owner.

To obtain permission(s) to use material from this work, please submit a written request to Pearson Higher Education, Rights and Contracts Department, 501 Boylston Street, Suite 900, Boston, MA 02116, or fax your request to 617-671-3447.

Library of Congress Cataloging-in-Publication Data

Brownell, Judi.
  What every student should know about listening /
    Judi Brownell, Andrew Wolvin.
      p. cm.
  ISBN 0-205-77807-0
  1. Attention.   2. Listening—Study and teaching (Higher)
  3. Communication in education.
  I. Wolvin, Andrew D. II. Title.
  LB1065.B7795 2010
  153.6'8—dc22
                                              2009038343

10   9   8   7   6   5   4   3   2   V013   13   12   11

**Allyn & Bacon
is an imprint of**

PEARSON

www.pearsonhighered.com

ISBN-10: 0-205-77807-0
ISBN-13: 978-0-205-77807-2

CONTENTS

Preface and Acknowledgments vi

CHAPTER 1: *Why Does Every Student Need to Know About Listening?* 1

Box 1.1. Relative Time Spent in Each Communication Activity 2

CHAPTER 2: *Why Is Listening so Important?* 4

Listening Is How We Connect with Others 4

Listening Helps Accomplish Tasks 5

Listening Improves Your Personal Well-Being 5

    Questions for Thought 6
    Things You Can Do Now 6
    Pre-Self-Assessment Instrument 7

CHAPTER 3: *Identify Your Listening Goals* 9

To Understand Messages 10

To Evaluate Messages 10

To Help Other People by Listening to Them 11

To Enjoy the Sights and Sounds Around You 11

To Distinguish Among Various Stimuli 11

Listening Goals Are Reciprocal and Not Mutually Exclusive 12

    Questions for Thought 12
    Things You Can Do Now 13

CHAPTER 4: *How Listening Works* 14

Figure 4.1. The Listening Chain 15

Receive Messages 15

Understand Messages 16

Remember Messages 16

Interpret Messages 17

Evaluate Messages   18

Respond Appropriately to Messages   18
   Questions for Thought   19
   Things You Can Do Now   19

CHAPTER 5: *The Art of Paying Attention*   20

Willingness to Listen—Motivation   21

Box 5.1. The LAW of Listening   21

Distractions—How You Can Handle Them   21
   External Distractions   22
   Internal Distractions   22

How You Influence Your Listening Effectiveness   22

Situational Influences on Your Attention   23
   Questions for Thought   24
   Things You Can Do Now   24

CHAPTER 6: *How to Achieve Your Listening Goals: Put Those Skills into Practice*   26

Pay Attention—Make Sure You Receive the Message   26

Box 6.1. Avoid the Pitfalls to Receiving Messages   27

Get It Right   27

Box 6.2. Two Helpful Outline Methods   28

Develop Strategies to Trigger Recall When You Need it   29

Box 6.3. Avoid Misunderstandings   29

Use All Your Senses—Develop Sensitivity to Nonverbal Messages   31

Box 6.4. Remember the Messages You Receive   31

Box 6.5. Nonverbal Cues that Say, "I'm Listening"   32

Box 6.6. Voice Conveys Emotions   32

Box 6.7. Listen Beyond Words to Interpret Messages   33

Think Critically—Don't Let Your Emotions Rule   33

Choose an Appropriate Listening Response   34

Box 6.8. Listen Critically   34

Box 6.9. Choose an Appropriate Listening Response   36

Questions for Thought   36
Things You Can Do Now   37

CHAPTER 7: *How to Listen Wherever You Are*   38

Listening One-on-One   38
   Questions for Thought   39
   Things You Can Do Now   39

Listening in Small Groups   40
   Questions for Thought   40
   Things You Can Do Now   41

Listening to Lectures   41
   Questions for Thought   42
   Things You Can Do Now   42

CHAPTER 8: *Listening Challenges You Might Face*   43

Listening to Those Who Have Different Cultural Orientations   43
   Questions for Thought   44
   Things You Can Do Now   44

Gender and Listening   45
   Questions for Thought   46
   Things You Can Do Now   46

Listening with Technology   47
   Questions for Thought   48
   Things You Can Do Now   48

Listening When Confronted with Ethical Dilemmas   48
   Questions for Thought   49
   Things You Can Do Now   50

CHAPTER 9: *Develop Your Action Plan*   51

Before You Listen   51

As You Listen   52

After You Listen   52
   Questions for Thought   53
   Things You Can Do Now   53
   Post-Self-Assessment Instrument   54

CHAPTER 10: *Where Do You Go from Here?*   57

PREFACE

What do you know about listening? Have you had a course in the subject? Do you talk about listening challenges and accomplishments with your friends and classmates? If you are like most other college students, this is probably not a subject you spend a lot of time thinking about. That's why many of the ideas in ***What Every Student Should Know About . . . Listening*** may be new to you. You probably think of speaking as the "hard part" of communication, and you probably sit in your classes expecting your professors to "tell you" everything you need to know. This perspective results in a lot of lost information, sometimes poor grades, and definitely a less exciting and stimulating communication experience! After reading this booklet, you will discover that increased attention to listening results in more satisfying relationships, fewer misunderstandings, and significantly improved personal well-being.

ACKNOWLEDGMENTS

The authors would like to thank all those students who, over many years of teaching and training, have broadened their understanding of the important role listening plays in the learning process. Colleagues, particularly those who come together in the International Listening Association to share ideas and insights, have also contributed to the content of this booklet. The writing process was greatly facilitated by the assistance of Rebecca Daniel, Cornell University, whose keen eye and thoughtful suggestions were much appreciated.

1

WHY DOES EVERY STUDENT NEED TO KNOW ABOUT LISTENING?

Like most students, you probably think that listening is automatic—if you think about it at all. In most cases, listening is something that you take for granted, that you "just do" without much thought or effort. This inaccurate view of listening, however, leads to numerous problems and frustrations in school as well as in your personal and professional relationships.

Actually, listening is one of the most important and most complex skills you will ever learn. Not only will effective listening help you succeed while you are in college, but you will also discover that good listeners are in demand in the workplace—in counseling, sales, education, engineering, health care, and many other professions. Effective listening is also recognized and appreciated in the situations we often take for granted as talking with friends and family.

Perhaps one reason why listening is so often taken for granted is that you do so much of it. Studies have repeatedly shown that when you are in college, you spend more of your time listening than you do reading, writing, or speaking. In fact, research suggests we may listen to as much as a book a day and speak the equivalent of a book a week. College students may spend nearly 60 percent of their communication time functioning as listeners.

Only when you stop for a minute and think about the variety of ways in which you listen does the importance and pervasiveness of listening become evident. While you are very conscious of the hours you spend reading a book or the fifteen minutes it takes to respond to your e-mail, the constant listening that you do goes

Relative Time Spent in Each Communication Activity

Listening	first
Speaking	second
Reading	third
Writing	fourth

largely unrecognized. If you were suddenly asked to make an oral presentation, you would worry about remembering your ideas and doing a good job. How about when you know you will be in a situation where you have to listen? Do you feel the same sense of concern and anxiety? Probably not. Listening, for most people, is considered a passive and covert process. Who knows if you are really listening?

Scholars have confirmed that, to be an effective listener, you must be actively engaged in the activity. In other words, listening well takes effort and a lot of hard work. You may have heard the term *active listening* being used to distinguish this deliberate and purposeful process. Since listening is such a central part of both your college success and your more general life experiences, it is useful to examine the process more closely. Listening skills can be learned and improved, so the sooner you begin, the more quickly you will reap the benefits.

As a listener, then, you must step up and take responsibility for the outcome of your communication. In fact, begin now assuming that *most* of the responsibility for successful communication rests with you as the listener. This perspective, putting more emphasis on the listener's role, is undoubtedly a major change from the way most people think about the communication process. You've probably always assumed that listening is the passive part of communication. You might have thought that all you had to do, essentially, was to show up! It was the speaker who had to do the work to make sure the message was clear and to keep you engaged and focused. You'll discover that's just not true—listeners work equally hard, if not harder, than speakers during the communication process.

Good listening requires several basic ingredients: (1) that you recognize its importance to you personally so that you will be motivated to listen well, (2) that you identify your listening goals so that you can work to achieve them, (3) that you understand the listening process itself so that you can identify the skills you'll need to develop in order to accomplish your objectives, and (4) that you continuously apply and practice listening behaviors that will increase your effectiveness in a variety of listening contexts. These topics, then, are what this book is all about.

2

Why Is Listening so Important?

No one can tell you exactly how listening will benefit you now and in the years to come, but it might help to think of the advantages you derive as falling into three general categories.

Listening Is How We Connect with Others

Human beings connect with one another through the stories they tell. Think about the most memorable listening experiences you have had. They probably center on the wonderful stories that someone told in a lecture, in a conversation, in a meeting, or on television. We all carry narratives in our long-term memories, and we tap into those stories as we process others' points, arguments, examples, and expressions. It's how we resonate with our friends, family, and even faculty members.

Think about the person you go to when you have a problem or when you need help making an important decision. If you were to identify this person's characteristics, chances are good that you would describe him or her as an effective listener. We all find it easier to get to know people who focus on what we say, give us encouragement, and let us express ourselves without interrupting or judging our ideas. These are the people we respect and whose opinions we trust.

Relationships are built through repeated sharing of information in an honest and straightforward manner. You might think about effective listening as contributing to building trust, developing empathy, and generating respect. Listening, in many cases, is one of the most valuable gifts you can give as it demonstrates your concern and support for others.

Listening Helps Accomplish Tasks

When you listen well, you get things right. Whether focusing on what your professor says in class or on directions to a new restaurant, listening helps you accomplish your work and avoid costly misunderstandings. When you are confident that you understand, you are able to act with more conviction and self-confidence. Think of the numerous times someone has misunderstood your explanations or paid too little attention to instructions or advice. Sometimes the consequence is minor, like when you end up on the wrong street or when you get the wrong lunch order. In other cases, however, poor listening costs lives. As the world becomes smaller and we interact more frequently with classmates and colleagues from other countries and cultures, the challenge of working together effectively becomes even greater. We accomplish most of our daily tasks working with other people, and listening is essential when we need to coordinate our activities.

Listening Improves Your Personal Well-Being

Effective listeners also enjoy greater mental health and experience less stress than their non-listening peers. Think of the occasions when you have been weary or upset. What do you do? Listening to relaxing music, taking a walk in a quiet place, enjoying the sounds of nature—these listening activities are calming and restore your peace of mind. Surrounding yourself with soothing sounds takes little effort but has tremendous payoff in terms of both psychological and physical benefits.

We will repeatedly mention these three broad benefits as we look more closely at the listening process and what it means to be an effective listener.

Questions for Thought

1. How is listening important to you in your daily experiences?
2. How much time do you spend listening each day?
3. When does listening *really matter* to you?
4. How might effective listening contribute to your personal well-being?
5. How did you first "learn" to listen?

Things You Can Do Now

1. Identify people who must listen as part of their job. Talk with them about listening and find out how they learned to listen well.
2. Try to keep track of every time you rely on one of your best friends (or family members) listening to you. How often does this occur?
3. Every day for a week, take five minutes and jot down the range of things you have listened to that day. Then, next to each item, put a "5" if you were a highly effective listener down to a "1" if you didn't pay much attention. In another column, put a "5" next to each item that is extremely important and a lower number, down to "1," for less important listening situations. Are the two numbers—representing effectiveness and importance—similar or different? Where are the largest gaps?
4. As you start your journey to discover more about yourself as a listener, go through this assessment instrument and check your score. This pre–self-assessment can be useful to you as you think about what to apply and how to apply the suggestions we offer to help you become a better listener.

Assess Yourself As a Listener

Many students assume that they are good listeners because it seems to come naturally to them. The best way to really know how you listen, however, is to examine the skills involved in good listening more closely.

Take a look at the following assessment and complete as many of the questions as you can. Be honest—that's the only way you will know what you ne ed to do to improve! After reading **What Every Student Should Know About . . . Listening**, go over the questions again and see if you have changed your mind about any of the items. This list should also be helpful to you as you establish and work toward your personal listening goals after you learn more about the listening process.

	(4 pts) Not at all like me	(3 pts) A little bit like me	(2 pts) A lot like me	(1 pt) Just like me
1. My friends remember things a lot better than I do.	☐	☐	☐	☐
2. I frequently get distracted or daydream in class.	☐	☐	☐	☐
3. Because I don't think a person's background or past experiences are relevant in communication, I take what someone says at face value.	☐	☐	☐	☐
4. When I argue with a classmate or friend, I focus on winning my point.	☐	☐	☐	☐
5. If I don't know a word someone uses, I figure one word won't really matter anyway.	☐	☐	☐	☐

(Continued)

6. In a class situation, there's no point in giving any feedback. ☐ ☐ ☐ ☐

7. If I'm not interested in the subject, I can't make myself listen. ☐ ☐ ☐ ☐

8. I don't worry about remembering things—if it's important, someone will tell me again. ☐ ☐ ☐ ☐

9. If I have expertise, I give friends my advice whether they ask for it or not. ☐ ☐ ☐ ☐

10. I leave it to the speaker to make sure the message is accurate and logical. ☐ ☐ ☐ ☐

11. I find nonverbal communication can be misleading, so I try not to let a speaker's body language distract me from what they are saying. ☐ ☐ ☐ ☐

12. If a lecture is too hard to understand, I just tune out. ☐ ☐ ☐ ☐

3

IDENTIFY YOUR LISTENING GOALS

If you know why you are in school taking classes, and what you will do with the knowledge and skills you learn when you graduate, chances are that you will be motivated to do well. The same is true of listening. You listen for a variety of reasons, and clarifying your listening goal will help you to focus and improve. Sometimes, however, your goal may not be clear to you at first but develops during the activity itself. You may think you are going to listen to a dull, required speaker, but then discover that the presentation is funny and entertaining. You might, on the other hand, think that you will be hearing a trivial and light-hearted speech, but find instead that you learned valuable and interesting information. Or, you might be walking to class and suddenly realize that you are surrounded by sounds you hadn't noticed before.

There are hundreds of reasons to listen, but most objectives fall into one of five broad listening goals:

1. To understand messages.
2. To evaluate messages.
3. To help other people by listening to them.
4. To enjoy the sights and sounds around you.
5. To distinguish among various stimuli.

To Understand Messages

A central goal of almost all listening is to understand, what you might have heard referred to as *listening comprehension.* Listening comprehension is critical to a successful college experience; obviously, unless you understand what you hear in class you won't be able to retain and use the information when you need it. Much of the listening you do is with the goal of understanding the course material in order to do well on tests and, hopefully, use and apply the information in the future. If you misunderstand instructions for an exam, or aren't able to follow oral directions to an event, the consequences can be serious.

We also rely on listening comprehension to understand advice from counselors, instructions from internship supervisors, and friends' suggestions. If you plan to take action on what others advise you to do, it's essential for you to accurately understand their intended meanings.

To Evaluate Messages

The next goal is to listen critically to evaluate and analyze the substance of a message. Through this process, you determine the value and accuracy of what you hear, and decide whether you agree with the speaker. This is a particularly appropriate listening goal if the message is persuasive and warrants a critical analysis. We're exposed to as many as three thousand persuasive messages during any given day, so it's important to have criteria by which to judge the merits of efforts to convince us to change what we believe, how we behave, or the ideas we support.

To be effective, the critical listener must first listen with careful comprehension in order to fully understand the message before deciding its merits. Unfortunately, we too often form premature or even unnecessary judgments on occasions when critical listening should not be our first listening response. As you'll soon discover, evaluating messages is one of several key listening skills used in combination with understanding and interpreting messages.

To Help Other People by Listening to Them

Another important purpose of listening is to provide a sounding board for someone who needs to talk through a problem. What we often call *therapeutic* or *empathic* listening requires that you focus your full attention on the speaker to understand what he or she is attempting to communicate. Friends, roommates, even classmates may need a therapeutic listener—someone who will let them simply "vent" and talk about a problem or issue. Ideally, they will then be better able to resolve the problem. To be effective at therapeutic listening, you must set aside your personal bias and perspectives, refrain from giving advice, and focus entirely on serving as a sounding board so the speaker can talk through and think through the issues for himself or herself.

To Enjoy the Sights and Sounds Around You

Sometimes, it's good to listen and find enjoyment in the sounds around you. Listening to appreciate what you receive is very personal, because listening for enjoyment is different for each person and takes many forms—from listening at sports arenas to theaters to concert halls.

Listeners bring many different experiences and preferences to this type of listening. At the most basic level, you can enjoy listening as a sensory experience. You might exercise to the beat of background music in the gym or identify the sounds of nature during a walk in the woods. At a more sophisticated level, you may be able to appreciate great composers or the unique patterns of a foreign language. Whatever you enjoy, it is up to you to find as many opportunities as possible to experience sound as a way to increase your pleasure (and often reduce your stress as well).

To Distinguish Among Various Stimuli

Another fundamental and often unconscious goal is listening to distinguish among sounds and other sensory stimuli. Perhaps the best way to understand this type of listening is to identify those instances when you do it deliberately, for instance, when you "tune in" to the computer printer if you think it's malfunctioning, or when you listen attentively to determine if the noise you heard was a car coming down the driveway. In such cases, you try to differentiate the sounds you hear and distinguish those that are important and meaningful from those that are extraneous. If you have recently learned a foreign language, you know that the more familiar you become with the new language, the easier it is to hear the distinct sounds that comprise each new word.

Listening Goals Are Reciprocal and Not Mutually Exclusive

Your listening goals—to comprehend, provide support, evaluate, appreciate, or discriminate—are best accomplished when they are compatible with the speaker's communication goal. If you listen carefully early in the interaction, you should be able to discern his or her purpose. Think to yourself: Is it okay just to enjoy what I'm receiving, or do I have to assess its value? Is it important for me to thoroughly understand the speaker's ideas, or is it enough for me to remember the topics discussed? With this information, you can adjust your listening accordingly. Keep in mind that this requires you to listen *actively*—to work at accomplishing your listening goal.

There are many occasions when you might be listening for more than one purpose. Perhaps you are taking a music class and find yourself not only enjoying what you hear, but also discriminating to determine the various instruments that are playing the particular piece. You might also listen to understand the type of rhythm and determine the composer.

Questions for Thought

1. Give an example of a personal listening situation that falls into each of the five goal categories described.
2. What listening goals, at this point in time, matter most to you? Do you think that some are inherently more important than others? Explain.

3. How is your motivation or attitude affected by your specific listening goal?
4. Which goals generally give you the most pleasure? Which create the most stress?
5. Do you "prepare" to accomplish some listening goals? Is it possible to anticipate most listening situations you encounter?
6. What is the probable consequence when your listening goal and your partner's goal are in conflict? Give an example of where that has been the case.

Things You Can Do Now

1. Try to determine how you can measure your success in accomplishing an important listening goal.
2. Keep track of how much time you spend listening in each of the five categories described. Where do you spend most of your time? Are there any types of listening on which you could be placing more emphasis?
3. Notice how the situation or context influences your listening. Describe the type of environment that, you find, facilitates listening effectiveness.

4

HOW LISTENING WORKS

Each of the five listening purposes or goals just discussed requires you to listen in a slightly different way. This is because listening isn't a simple process. Rather, it depends upon a number of interrelated skills that can be clustered into six listening "links." You accomplish your listening goals by understanding each of the linked skill clusters, and then determining which links of the listening chain are most relevant to a given situation. Overall listening competence can only be achieved when you have improved your performance in each of the six links and have applied them appropriately to your specific needs.

We envision listening as a linking process. Each dimension of this complex process overlaps with the others in a very dynamic, ongoing way as one listens. If something disrupts the process (attention is diverted to a noise outside the classroom window), the link is temporarily broken until the listener regroups to link back into the listening experience. That linking process can be visualized as a "listening chain" (see Figure 4.1).

Listening improvement may sometimes seem like an overwhelming task. By focusing on one skill cluster at a time, however, you can identify and then work on the links that will make the most difference. Several of the links, or skill clusters, correspond closely to the listening goals just described. In almost all cases, however, you will need to excel in more than one listening "link" in order to accomplish your objectives. The skill clusters include receiving, understanding, remembering, interpreting, evaluating, and responding. Each is discussed in more detail in the following pages.

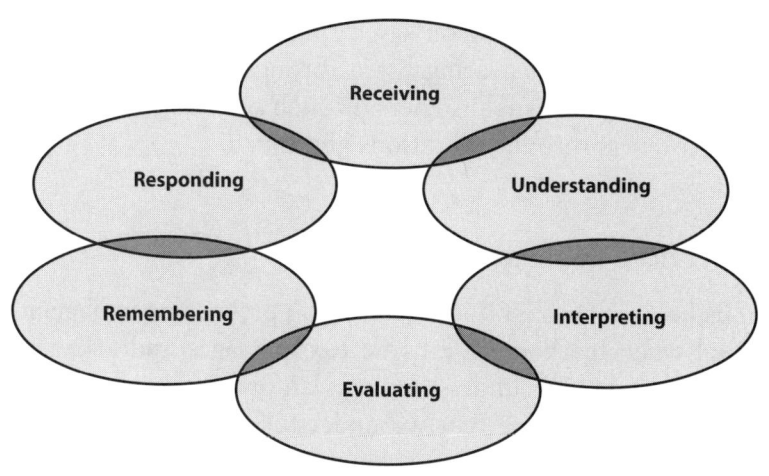

Figure 4.1. The Listening Chain

Receive Messages

It's easy to confuse *hearing* and *listening*—particularly because people often use the two terms interchangeably. There is, however, a big difference! Hearing is just the first step in the listening process. Hearing is the reception of sound through air waves—the physical process that involves the ear and its mechanical functioning. The next section discusses the importance of focusing attention and is closely related to listening; unless you pay attention to the right things, you will not hear the messages you need and little or no listening will take place.

Hearing varies from one person to the next, and changes over time. Those who are unable to hear well may find listening more difficult because they can only process information that has been clearly received.

It may surprise you to know that listening extends to the reception of other sensory stimuli, most particularly the visual message. Consider that the brain is wired to process visual stimuli more than anything. And consider how speakers are constantly sending visual messages through their body language, eye contact, and facial expressions. Indeed, you will learn when we discuss how messages are interpreted, what listeners receive visually may have the greatest impact. Your first impression of someone is probably formed before you ever hear that person say a single word. And students who are deaf or hard of hearing listen through the other sensory channels, especially as visual listeners through sign language and as kinesthetic listeners through vibrations and touch.

Understand Messages

Most of us became familiar with reading comprehension in elementary school when teachers gave us written passages and asked us questions to assess our understanding. Unfortunately, far fewer teachers checked to ensure that we understood the oral messages that we heard. Yet, particularly for you as a student, listening comprehension is not only an important listening goal but is also a key skill for your success. If you have classes in a foreign language, you learn new vocabulary so that you can understand what is said. Many times, however, vocabulary is taken for granted even though it is not shared. Those who are interested in math, for example, may use terms like *hypotenuse* or *theorem* and confuse their listeners. Technology is advancing quickly, and words like *Twitter* and *iPod* may be foreign to those who grew up in a world with fewer communication options.

Vocabulary also allows for greater precision and expression of ideas, and increases the accuracy of shared messages. Unless you know the meaning of a word, it is nearly impossible to share meanings and grasp the speaker's intent. As the world becomes more global, it is more likely that you will be communicating with friends and students from other countries, and a deliberate focus on understanding what you receive will be even more essential.

Remember Messages

What you experience is only useful if you can remember the information and put it to use. If you sit in class and pay attention to everything that is said—yet can't recall the information for an exam—your listening has not really been effective.

Good memories don't just happen. They are developed through training and, yes, hard work. We have discussed the importance of paying attention so that information is received; an equally important task is to store the ideas in your memory so that you can use what you learned at a later time. It is especially important for you, as a student, to be able to retrieve information and then apply it appropriately. You do this by using a variety of memory strategies that will help you move what you receive through your short-term memory into your long-term memory system.

Interpret Messages

After fully understanding the message, it is important to take an additional step—to interpret or make sense of the message in light of the specific speaker and situation. This stage of the listening process is more personal and subjective. It involves using nonverbal and contextual cues to augment the words you hear. Listeners often need to rely on their subjective perceptions and intuition as they screen each message in order to make sense of the information.

Because perceptual filters are shaped by previous life experiences, each listener interprets what he or she perceives in a slightly different manner. Your previous knowledge of the subject, your physical and emotional state, and your relationship with the speaker are just a few of the dimensions that influence how you view the world and, in turn, how you make sense of what you receive.

Nonverbal communication is a particularly important element in accurately interpreting messages. Often, a speaker's nonverbal messages will contradict his or her verbal statements. For instance, you may have been assigned to teams in class. The instructor says, "Jamie, would you mind if we put Nadia in your group?" You know Nadia is a poor student, unreliable, and constantly absent. It isn't hard, then, for you to notice that when Jamie says, "Sure, fine," her nonverbal communication suggests otherwise.

Facial expression, body posture, and eye contact all convey information that the effective listener notices and uses to more accurately interpret the speaker's meaning. Your cultural background is also an important factor as different behaviors—both verbal and nonverbal—have different meanings depending upon your cultural context.

Evaluate Messages

When you hear the word *evaluate*, it's likely that you think of something negative. You've probably been told things like, "Don't be judgmental," or "It's horrible to be evaluated!" Recall, however, that one of the most common and practical listening goals is to evaluate messages to determine the accuracy and value of each idea. Evaluate, in this context, means that you don't take what you receive at face value. Instead, you analyze the content and hold messages to the test of logic and reasoning. It has to do with your critical thinking ability and your willingness to take a few extra seconds to be thoughtful and disciplined so that you are not misled.

Often, speakers use emotional appeal and unfounded assumptions as they try to accomplish their persuasive aims. When someone tries to convince you to stay out late and not do your homework, or to let him or her borrow your car, it helps to step back and analyze the nature of the appeals he or she are using to convince you to see things from his or her point of view. Pausing long enough to recognize the logical fallacies or the emotionally charged persuasive strategies will help you make the best decision as a critical listener.

In the end, whether you agree with what the speaker is saying or not, it is up to you to consider the merit of the messages you receive.

Respond Appropriately to Messages

Your listening effectiveness is expressed directly or indirectly by the response you make to the messages you receive. Your communication partner only knows how well you listened by observing your reactions. If you think about it, you have nearly unlimited choices regarding your verbal and nonverbal responses. You could ask a question. You could show agreement. You could restate the speaker's point. You could look confused. You could show frustration or impatience. When you respond as a direct result of what you heard, it is usually considered "feedback." The speaker learns how effective he or she has been by what you say or do—by the feedback you provide.

Your feedback, then, becomes the primary "message" and the speaker moves into the role of listener. In actuality, anyone engaged in the communication process is both listening and speaking simultaneously; as you speak, you observe and respond to the listener's reactions. Rather than a turn-taking scenario, communicators are continuously engaged in a dynamic and reciprocal exchange.

Questions for Thought
1. Which skill cluster do you rely on the most as a student?
2. Which skill cluster do you believe is your weakest area?
3. Are there any other aspects of listening that aren't covered in the six skill clusters, which you use when you listen?

Things You Can Do Now
1. Keep a journal of your listening requirements and compare your first impression of the skill clusters you rely on with the results of your personal records. Were you accurate?
2. Search the phrase *memory techniques* on the Internet and identify some techniques that will be most helpful to you. Then practice them!
3. Identify the circumstances in which you have a hard time remaining objective and listening critically. Try to catch yourself jumping to unwarranted conclusions while you are in the listening situation.

5

THE ART OF PAYING ATTENTION

Before you can listen at all, you need to pay attention! In most cases, attention is a matter of choice. Where you focus your attention, and how much energy you decide to devote to a particular message and communication situation, influences the success of the encounter.

You probably think that you can focus your attention as long as you choose. Wrong! Research suggests that you can maintain attention for about thirty seconds at best before you need to refocus. As a result (and as you've probably noticed!), your attention fluctuates as you listen. Most of us listen for six to eight minutes and then take a "mini break." After forty-five minutes of listening, you are likely to be daydreaming or dozing off! A good listener will recognize when attention, energy, and interest are waning and do whatever is necessary to refocus and mentally reengage with the speaker. Research in listening suggests that we are more likely to attend to messages that are relevant, unique, and loud.

Another reason why it's difficult to maintain attention is that there is a considerable gap between the time it takes a speaker to express a thought, and the time it takes a listener to process that information and make it meaningful. This difference, often referred to as the "thought-speech gap," gives you as a listener so much free mental time that your mind begins to wander. The trick, as you will later learn, is to manage your bonus time to create a listening advantage.

Willingness to Listen — Motivation

More than anything else, attention depends on your motivation. If you are motivated, it will be much easier for you to pay attention to a speaker's message. Think of the times you have tuned out during a class because you didn't find it to be particularly interesting to you. Yet, you never know when what you hear may be important—much of the information that was ignored could show up on the final exam!

Essentially, then, a successful listener is a "willing" listener. You have to *want* to listen in order to listen well. It's important to set aside any negative messages that may block your listening, like: "This isn't interesting," or "I'm not a good listener," or "I've heard all of this before." Instead, willingness to listen shifts these messages to the positives: "I'm a good listener," "This may be important," "Perhaps there is something more I can learn." By giving yourself good reasons to listen, you will further facilitate effective communication.

Distractions — How You Can Handle Them

You just learned that before any listening can occur you need to focus your attention. There are literally hundreds of stimuli bombarding you at any given time, and many of them will affect your listening by distracting you from your listening objective. If you become more aware of these influences, you will be better able to manage them and increase the likelihood that you will be able to concentrate. It's also important, of course, to avoid as many distractions as possible. You might think of the things that distract you as either being inside or outside your head, and as either within or outside of your control.

The LAW of Listening

Listening = Ability + Willingness

External Distractions

Let's begin by taking a look at the external distractions you regularly face. Many of these are relatively easy to manage. Set aside your cell phone, iPod, or BlackBerry, and give your undivided attention to the speaker. Refuse to engage in side conversations with fellow classmates or friends when you are in a listening situation. Refrain from looking out the window or engaging in other tasks while listening. The skilled listener gives the speaker respect and attention.

Other external distractions include such things as the room temperature, noise in your surroundings, or other factors related to your general comfort and ability to focus and relax.

Internal Distractions

Internal distractions are often the most difficult to overcome. Perhaps you have an upcoming exam, or you just discovered that your best friend was coming to visit, or a loved one is ill. Sometimes it seems almost impossible to concentrate on the immediate communication—your focus keeps going back to these strong thoughts swirling in your mind. While all of this makes effective listening difficult, once again it is your job to reduce or eliminate distractions to the extent possible. The following tips will help you work toward this goal.

How You Influence Your Listening Effectiveness

Who you are influences what you pay attention to and, consequently, what you hear. How is that possible? Your values, past experiences, preferences, and the unique way in which you perceive and interpret stimuli affect your listening outcomes. Your mood, your interests, and other factors also contribute to individual differences in listening and can make your job either easier or more difficult. We call these variables *listening filters*, because everything you hear is "filtered" through your personal information-processing system.

Your attitude toward the speaker or the subject also can either inhibit or facilitate listening effectiveness. If you go into a listening situation with a positive outlook and expect to learn something, you have a much better chance of concentrating than if you make up your mind in advance that it will be a waste of your time. In addition, your attitude and relationship with the speaker influences your receptiveness and ability to accurately process what you hear. If you believe that a speaker has a great deal of credibility, you are likely to pay more attention to what he has to say. When friends tell you something, you *want* to believe them and you listen in a more open manner. A useful communication theory proposes that if you feel positively toward the speaker, you will want to share the speaker's view of the subject. If, however, you don't respect or if you dislike the speaker, you will feel most comfortable disagreeing with his or her position on the subject. See if you can apply this theory the next time you listen to a persuasive speech.

More general personal characteristics also affect how you listen and what you listen to most effectively. Your age and gender, for instance, influence your interests and listening choices. Would you choose to watch the same DVDs as one of your grandparents, or a neighbor who is just in kindergarten? We often use terms like *macho*, or *chick flick* to distinguish those movies likely to interest men and women, respectively. Gender, age, personal style, and cultural norms all influence the choices you make and your listening preferences.

All listeners are more effective if they are rested and healthy. You know when you haven't gotten any sleep or if you are sick how difficult it is to pay attention in class. Taking care of yourself so that you are rested and alert is prerequisite to being an effective communicator.

Situational Influences on Attention

When you find yourself having difficulty listening, take a look around. Often, your environment can be changed to make your job easier. Move chairs so you are closer to the speaker or take a seat in the front of the room. Make sure that you have enough light, that your seat is comfortable, and that you aren't by a window where you are more likely to be distracted. Construction going on outside your window, an air conditioner blasting on your shoulders, or the sounds of a noisy radiator all have the potential to distract you from listening effectively. Anticipate whether the room is likely to be hot or cold, and dress accordingly; if you know you will be hungry before a class is over, get something to eat ahead of time (yes, hunger interferes with listening!). Rather than simply accepting a difficult listening context, try to figure out if there is some way to reduce or eliminate distractions so that you can concentrate on the important listening activity.

Your reaction to the listening setting also affects your ability to listen well. Think of the difference between listening in your school's cafeteria and a courtroom, or between listening at the dining room table and at a sporting event. In each case, you need to change the amount of energy you spend as well as the techniques you use in order for communication to be successful.

Questions for Thought

1. Is there any way to tell for sure when you are speaking to someone who is distracted?
2. Should you tell the speaker if something is distracting you and you know you are not paying full attention to what is being said?
3. What is the speaker's responsibility for holding your attention as a listener? Is this the same for all situations?
4. Which do you find most difficult to overcome, internal or external distractions?
5. Do you think men and women are distracted by different things? Explain.
6. What are your most challenging listening environments with regard to distractions? Why?

Things You Can Do Now

1. For a week, keep a journal of the things that distract you in class. Then, next to each distraction, indicate how it could be overcome or reduced.
2. As you sit down for class, take a few seconds to focus on the preparation you did and on what you expect to hear that day.

3. Make sure you apply the tips that will help you focus your attention—sit close to the speaker, come to class with all the materials you will need to actively participate in the session, and so forth.
4. As you're listening to a lecture, stop periodically and quickly jot down what you're concentrating on at that moment. At the end of class, check your list and see where your attention wandered. Try to determine why you were affected by these particular distractions.

6

How to Achieve Your Listening Goals: Put Those Skills into Practice

In addition to clarifying your listening goals and identifying the six components of the listening process, effective listeners also adopt attitudes and practice specific behaviors that will facilitate and constantly improve their skills. While several of the following items should sound familiar by now, they warrant repeating. When you learn and focus on the key components of listening competence, you will be in the best position to ensure that you have a positive and productive listening experience.

Pay Attention—Make Sure You Receive the Message

Key skill cluster: Receiving

Now you know that one of the first things you can do to improve your listening is to get yourself into a position where you can see and hear the speaker. This may require that you not sit at the back of the classroom or by a window. As discussed earlier, managing your physical environment includes such things as avoiding side conversations and putting away your cell phone or laptop. While some distractions are beyond your individual control, it's your responsibility to make every effort to manage the situation so that you maximize your listening effectiveness.

Research suggests that physical exercise is important to cognitive ability. Other health-related research reinforces the need for

> **Avoid the Pitfalls to Receiving Messages**
> - Be ready—prepare to listen
> - Don't interrupt the speaker
> - Don't fake attention
> - Identify personal factors that interfere with paying attention

the human body to have enough sleep in order to function properly; never underestimate the importance of having rest. Exercise and diet impact the way you function as a listener. If you care about your listening effectiveness, you will schedule enough time to satisfy these basic needs so that you are alert physically and mentally, and able to get the most value from each listening situation.

Get it Right

Key skill cluster: Understanding

There are numerous things you can do to increase your chances of avoiding misunderstandings—of "getting it right." Before class, you should read the text chapters, handouts, and assignments thoroughly so that you'll have the necessary background to understand whatever is discussed during the class period.

Study any new vocabulary words so that any terms specific to the topic will be familiar to you as you listen. Increasingly, each discipline has its own words, and often they are used in a particular way. Know that OJT means on-the-job training, or that a roux is a thickening agent of flour and fat used in French cooking. Communication frequently breaks down because listeners are reluctant to ask for the meaning of a particular word or acronym. Wordsmith.com offers a "Word A Day" to help listeners increase their vocabulary.

You will find that taking notes helps you better understand and make sense of the speaker's lecture. In addition to traditional outlining methods, there are many other simple and effective note-taking strategies that will keep you focused on the lecture and assist with your listening comprehension. Two of these methods, concept versus fact and mapping, are described in the following box.

> ## Two Helpful Outline Methods
>
> **Concept Versus Fact Method**
>
> Draw a vertical line down the center of your paper. Whenever you hear a main concept, note it on the left side of the line. Record the facts that support this concept on the right side. That way, when you study, you will be able to distinguish between main points and the evidence or detail that supports them.
>
> **Mapping Method**
>
> This technique involves organizing what you hear visually on your paper so that you can see relationships among the various ideas presented. Record the main ideas in the center of your page, and leave room to jot down supporting information on the sides. Connect the details to the main points with lines which will radiate out from the center.

You can also increase your ability to listen when visuals are involved. Effective speakers will put simple bullets on PowerPoint slides and use them to visually reinforce and clarify the points as they talk about each of them. "Death by PowerPoint" speakers, however, will put long and detailed text on slides so that you essentially have to stop listening and become a reader to deal with all of the detailed information. If you're in a class where the instructor doesn't use PowerPoint effectively, you'll need to make decisions as to what will be most productive—to focus attention on the slides and copy some of the material, or to focus on the speaker's oral message.

Ideally, the professor will give you a handout of the PowerPoint slides in a format that provides lines for taking notes in the right-hand column on the page. This can facilitate your taking notes, because you don't have to frantically copy down what's on the slide before the next slide is projected. And you can be more focused on the professor's lecture because you don't have to worry about having to get the details down on paper.

Slightly different techniques work to improve your comprehension in one-on-one listening situations. One of the most effective means of insuring accurate understanding is to ask questions! Too frequently, we let the moment pass and then never go back to check on information we might have missed. Regardless of whether you are talking with your instructor or your best friend, questions show that you care about getting things right.

Another helpful method to increase comprehension is to use a paraphrase, or to restate what you believe are the speaker's main points. By reflecting ideas back to your communication partner you not only surface any misunderstandings, but you also provide an opportunity for the speaker to clarify and subsequently modify his or her thoughts.

Paraphrasing is particularly helpful in situations where someone gives you directions or asks you to perform a specific task. By acknowledging the request and restating your intentions you find out about the accuracy of your understanding in a timely and efficient manner.

Develop Strategies to Trigger Recall When You Need It

Key skill cluster: Remembering

Did you know that you probably remember only 20 percent of what you hear, but 30 percent of what you see? Consequently, good listeners learn and implement strategies for triggering recall so that they can make the best use of their memory system. They concentrate and mentally consider the speaker's points so that they can use the information at a later date, either when they go to take a quiz or when they intend to keep a promise.

Avoid Misunderstandings

- Increase your vocabulary
- Ask questions
- Restate your understanding through perception checks
- Focus on main ideas as well as details

Keep in mind that one of the most common reasons why you have trouble remembering what was said is because you didn't really pay attention in the first place. When introduced to someone in a social situation, for instance, you might be thinking about what is going on elsewhere in the room or on what witty remark you will make to impress the person. These mental tangents keep you from hearing the person's name. Instead, look directly at the person. Repeat their name, and use it again within a few minutes. You will find that it is much easier to remember when you see them the next day in a grocery store!

We first capture messages in our short-term or "working memory." Unless we do something to store this information for later use, it is quickly lost. That's why you may benefit from practicing memory techniques that help you transfer the "input" you hear into meaningful information—and then get it back when you need it!

Effective listeners develop an arsenal of memory strategies. Simple associations are one way you can improve your memory—think about where you saw that beautiful house or what other movies have featured a particular actress. Sometimes, the more outrageous the image, the better. Remember to get ice cream at the grocery store by visualizing the entire aisle dripping with hot fudge—when you leave your car keys on top of the computer, think of the monitor as a face with the keys hanging on an imagined nose. Mnemonic techniques are another type of memory aid; they require that you create visual images that will help you retrieve what you heard at a later date. A familiar example is HOMES, the acronym for remembering the Great Lakes (Huron, Ontario, Michigan, Erie, and Superior).

Many students discover that chunking techniques, breaking down large amounts of information into small bits and rehearsing them over and over until you're able to readily recall them, are helpful in preparing for class and for tests. Memory development specialists note that writing down key points and keeping a list may be one of the best memory strategies for recall. The act of writing notes while listening taps into your kinesthetic sense, makes use of the visual channel on the page, and reinforces what you're receiving so that you can remember the information later when you need it.

While sometimes you might feel that remembering more will cause you to forget what you already know, just the opposite is true. Think of your brain as a supercomputer, a large information processor with nearly unlimited capacity. As we receive the message, we seek a match in the verbal and/or nonverbal language banks already stored in our long-term memory. If there is no match, the message may be sent back, cognitively, for a second-level analysis, or it may simply be discarded because we have no frame of reference for understanding it. In other words, the more you study and the more knowledgeable you become, the easier it is to learn new information!

Use All Your Senses — Develop Your Sensitivity to Nonverbal Messages

Key skill cluster: Interpreting

Listening to words isn't the only way to gather important information. As you know from reading the previous section, a speaker's nonverbal communication also provides important cues to help you interpret, or give meaning, to the messages you receive. When you consider unique characteristics of the person who is speaking and the context in which communication takes place, you will be more likely to accurately understand the speaker's intended meaning.

Those with a high level of sensitivity to nonverbal messages are said to have "emotional intelligence." An emotionally intelligent listener pays attention to the speaker's facial expression and body posture and uses these cues to create a more comprehensive understanding of the situation. They notice when a friend or coworker seems stressed or tired, and take that into account when they determine the speaker's intended meaning.

Remember the Messages You Receive
- Distinguish facts from main ideas—try to see the big picture
- Learn and practice specific long-term memory strategies
- Focus on the message, not on yourself

> **Nonverbal Cues that Say, "I'm Listening"**
> - Direct eye contact
> - Positive facial expression
> - Periodic nods
> - Touching
> - Forward body orientation

Tone of voice also provides clues to the speaker's emotional state. When someone is nervous or giddy or upset or frustrated, it will often change the way he or she speaks. Voice can vary on several dimensions, including rate (fast and slow), pitch (high and low), and volume (loud and soft). If someone is stressed, for instance, his or her voice may be higher and the rate faster than normal. Vocal cues are so powerful, in fact, that most listeners find them more reliable indicators of the speaker's emotional state than what the individual says about his or her feelings. Keep in mind, too, that silence also communicates. If you ask your friends to borrow their notes, or take a look at their homework, their silence may convey the answer more clearly than words.

In addition, good listeners find out about the speaker's background and past experiences to determine if these factors have an influence on their attitudes and behavior. Recognizing, for instance, that someone just broke up with his fiancée or that the transmission went bad in the car he just bought can help you put his ideas and responses into perspective. If your friend failed her biology test and is upset and worried, it will affect her interactions and attitudes.

> **Voice Conveys Emotions**
>
> | | Volume | Pitch | Rate |
> |--------|----------|----------|------|
> | **Joy** | loud | high | fast |
> | **Sorrow** | soft | low | slow |
> | **Apathy** | moderate | moderate | slow |

> **Listen Beyond Words to Interpret Messages**
> - Observe the speaker's body language and eye behavior
> - Listen carefully to the speaker's voice for clues to how he or she feels
> - Determine what silence may mean
> - Consider the speaker's background, values, attitudes, and past experiences

Think Critically—Don't Let Your Emotions Rule

Key skill cluster: Evaluating

Another key to effective listening is to recognize your emotional responses and make sure they don't lead you astray as you strive to objectively assess the messages you hear. As listeners, we all have our "hot buttons"—topics and words that set us off. Phrases such as "You *never* let me decide," "It's not my job," or "Yeah, just like a teenager" have the potential to create defensiveness and, subsequently, to undermine our efforts to listen critically. It's helpful to know what triggers your emotions and to make every effort to get past them so that you can be fair and accurate in assessing the value of a speaker's point.

The trick is to catch yourself jumping to conclusions or prejudging the value of a topic. There's nothing wrong with making an assessment of what you hear; the problem comes when you evaluate too quickly and do not remain open-minded. You have probably had the experience of being in an argument with someone and finding yourself just waiting for them to finish their sentence and take a breath so that you could get in your points. At that moment, are you listening? Probably not. Is this person listening to you? Probably not. You are falling into the trap of making "winning the argument" your goal rather than "learning new information" and arriving at the best conclusion.

You are also well served by identifying any emotional appeals that the speaker is using to convince you of his or her ideas. By surfacing these appeals, you will be reducing his or her impact and increasing the chances that your decision will be based on the facts of the situation. Regardless of the topic, it's good practice to ask yourself several key questions that will test the speaker's logic and reasoning. Among the most useful are:

1. What evidence is there to support this statement? Is it sufficient?
2. What is the source of the evidence? Is it recent and credible?
3. Has the speaker selected only information that supports his or her point, or are the facts representative of the situation?
4. Has the speaker exaggerated in any way?
5. Does the speaker have ulterior motives—does he or she derive personal benefit by being persuasive?

As we are bombarded daily with thousands of messages, it is important to take a critical perspective and automatically subject what you hear to simple tests of logic and reasoning. You will quickly discover that you are readily able to assess a speaker's ideas and that you will make better decisions as a result of this important skill.

Choose an Appropriate Listening Response

Key skill cluster: Responding

The way you respond to what a speaker says lets the person know whether or not you have listened well. Most of us have habitual ways of responding in certain situations. You might be quiet when a friend says something thoughtless to you, or get upset and argue

---

Listen Critically

- Recognize your emotional "triggers" and the speaker's emotional appeals
- Analyze logic and reasoning
- Listen to "learn," not to "win"
- Identify your own bias

when your parents disagree with your plans. It's important to recognize, however, that every response is a deliberate choice and that changing the type of response you make changes the dynamics of the communication and affects your future relationship with the other person.

Imagine your roommate says to you, "I lost my keys!" How might you respond?

> You could ask a question: "Where did you go after you got out of the car?"
>
> You could give advice: "Why don't you look in the car—I'll bet they fell under the seat."
>
> You could be supportive: "I'm so sorry! Don't worry, we'll find them."
>
> You could be judgmental: "I can't believe you lost them again!"
>
> You could ignore the statement: "Hey, do you want to go to a movie tonight?"

You could say nothing verbally but rather communicate nonverbally with a sympathetic look.

As you can see, each response will elicit a different reaction from the speaker and change the nature of your interaction. Effective listeners provide a response, or feedback, that is supportive and sensitive. Make sure your verbal and nonverbal responses are appropriate to the communication situation so that your feedback will further the communication goals that have been established. If you communicate a negative response, for example, you run the risk of shutting down the communication by alienating the speaker.

Remember, too, that you are always responding nonverbally—you cannot not communicate. Again, the key point is that you have choices and it is important for you to recognize how you are responding and to consider the connection between your listening response and the effectiveness of the communication.

Think about how you can best send the message, "I'm listening." Do you want to reinforce your interest by maintaining strong eye contact with the speaker? You can also let him or her know by your posture, facial expression, and other body language that you're focused on what he or she is saying and that it's important

> **Choose an Appropriate Listening Response**
> - Recognize your habitual response and determine if it is appropriate
> - Experiment with a variety of responses so you are comfortable in all situations
> - Let the speaker know that you are listening through both your verbal and nonverbal behavior

to you. Speakers appreciate listeners who are engaged and responsive, and this is particularly true in classroom settings where it is easy to become distracted.

You can see that listening takes both thought and work. To be successful, you need to become aware of exactly what you're doing, be willing to fully engage in the listening process, and acquire strategies that will increase your effectiveness. In fact, some listening experts believe that if you behave like a good listener, the attentiveness will actually help you to listen more effectively.

Questions for Thought

1. What listening situations do you find most challenging?
2. How would you rate your sensitivity to nonverbal cues? Do you think that this sensitivity, or emotional intelligence, can be learned?
3. What nonverbal behaviors are you particularly aware of in your professors? What do they do that helps keep you engaged? What do they do that you find distracting?
4. As a student, do you see yourself as a critical listener, or do you pretty much listen and accept what you hear without question?
5. When you were growing up, how much emphasis was placed on listening? What "messages" did you hear about the importance of listening from your parents and other adults?
6. How comfortable do you feel asking questions in class? When you are confused about something that is said, how do you go about getting things straightened out?

Things You Can Do Now

1. Keep a journal of your listening experiences. Try to record entries at least twice each day for a week.
2. Use your journal entries to determine the type of listening you do most, and the listening skills that you use most frequently.
3. Try to become more aware of how your classmates and friends listen. Who is one of the best listeners? What does he or she do? How does his or her behavior affect your interactions with him or her? Consider letting him or her know that you think he or she listens well.
4. What are some of your poor listening habits? Do you interrupt, or get bored easily? Ask a friend to let you know when you begin to fall into these habits. Catching yourself "in the act" is the first step to improving your listening.
5. Are there any students who are hard of hearing at your school? What resources are available to the hearing impaired? Find out more about how those who are challenged gather information.
6. Interview one of your professors and ask if he or she does anything intentionally to hold students' attention. Ask him or her to share experiences that he or she has had in the classroom with students who have trouble listening.

7
How to Listen Wherever You Are

You now know how important it is to identify your listening goals and to work on improving your effectiveness in each of the six skill clusters that together comprise listening competence. The importance of each listening component varies, of course, depending upon not only your goals, but also the context in which listening occurs. Three of the most frequent settings in which you will find yourself as a listener are one-on-one, small groups, and lectures. We illustrate how the principles discussed earlier are applied to these three listening contexts.

Listening One-on-One

The most casual yet meaningful listening likely occurs in one-on-one situations. You have lunch with a friend, you sit down next to a roommate in the student lounge, you meet up with a classmate and head to the library. While you would imagine that one-on-one listening would be simple, this type of listening is perhaps the most taken for granted. Therefore, additional effort can make biggest considerable difference in your listening effectiveness.

Since you have "full access" to one other person in a conversation, your opportunity for interpreting and adapting to messages is greatest in this context. You can observe the other person's nonverbal communication, provide continuous feedback, and use what you know about the individual's background and past experiences to fully understand his meaning. This focus also increases trust, as the person speaking realizes that you are concerned and interested in sharing ideas and fully understanding what you hear by depending on both verbal and nonverbal cues.

In addition to interpreting your partner's nonverbal cues, your eye contact and other nonverbal behavior is an important factor in facilitating positive outcomes. Nodding your head, leaning forward, and focusing on the person speaking will assure them that you understand and care about what they have to say. Such reinforcement is essential when your goal is to support or help the other person work through a problem or dilemma.

Listening one-on-one also gives you the best opportunity to ask questions and check your understanding. If you seek help from your instructor outside of class, asking questions for clarification and restating requirements will help assure that you do not misinterpret what is expected. This behavior also communicates to the person speaking that you are interested in getting things right.

Questions for Thought

1. What psychological and practical barriers do you experience when it comes to perception checking? Can you eliminate any of them?
2. When you are in one-on-one situations with different people, does your listening change? What differences are there between listening to a parent, a friend, or a teacher?
3. What can the speaker do to increase your listening effectiveness when you are talking one-on-one?
4. What behaviors do you display that either facilitate or hinder communication effectiveness? For instance, do you interrupt the speaker? Do you provide meaningful feedback?

Things You Can Do Now

1. What one-on-one listening situations do you take for granted? Make a list and, after each, indicate the level of your effectiveness.
2. What listening situations do you enter well prepared? Make a list of the things you do to prepare as a listener.

3. What nonverbal behaviors do you regularly display when you listen in one-on-one situations? Make a list, and then ask a friend this question. See if you are accurate in your self-perceptions.

Listening in Small Groups

As a student, you probably find yourself in a lot of small groups: social groups of friends or family, study groups to review for an upcoming exam, and project groups to complete a research assignment for a class. Small groups are often characterized by unequal participation among members. One person might do a lot of talking; another group member might be text messaging during the entire session! Often, team members think that the more they talk, the more helpful they are to the group. But who is listening? Many great ideas have been lost or never surfaced because one or two people dominated the conversation and other members chose not to speak because they felt that no one cared about what they had to say.

It doesn't matter if you are the team leader or one of several participants, you can help the team share information, collaborate, and reach its goal by actively listening. Is there someone who is quiet but who looks like he or she has something to say? Demonstrate your empathy and ask him or her what he or she is thinking. Is someone making unsubstantiated assumptions? Demonstrate your critical listening skills and question their conclusion by asking for additional support and evidence. Perhaps someone is going off on a tangent and distracting the team from its goal. Ask a question that refocuses members on the primary goal or topic. As you listen closely, you will be in the best position to recognize what the team needs in order to get its job accomplished.

Questions for Thought

1. Do you know of someone who seldom listens in small group settings? How does this behavior impact the team and its effectiveness?
2. Do you think that teams that have been assigned a task should talk only about the task, or should some time be spent on more social interactions? Explain.
3. Do you think an effective team leader needs to talk a lot, or can he or she mostly listen and be influential? Explain.

Things You Can Do Now

1. List the ways in which you might project empathy and help a team accomplish its goal without expressing your personal ideas. Try out these behaviors the next time you are in a group.
2. If you think back to your recent team experiences, who is your favorite team member? What does he or she do (or not do) that makes him or her fun to work with? Describe their listening behavior and determine if there is anything you can learn from him or her to improve your own performance.
3. The next time you are in a team situation, notice how various member behaviors either encourage or discourage your contribution to the discussion. Write down what team members said or did that facilitated information sharing, and what they did that inhibited you from participating.

Listening to Lectures

Recall how important motivation is to effective listening. If you go into a lecture thinking that the content is dull or the instructor is boring, you are doomed to not listen well. Instead, keep thinking about how you might be able to use what you are learning. Perhaps your physics class doesn't hold much interest for you now, but think about all of the applications there might be when you become a homeowner and have to fix appliances or do other maintenance activities. Don't let yourself daydream; stay involved by taking notes and using that mental "bonus" time to reflect on the subject matter.

Remember, too, that it's impossible to listen well if you're sitting next to someone who is surfing the Web or using an iPhone. Prepare to listen by reducing as many distractions as possible and by focusing your full attention on what is going on in the classroom.

As a student, you are also going to need to remember what you hear! Good notes that you can refer to later, and clearly organized ideas, will aid in recall. You have to "do something" with the information to get it from short-term into your long-term memory. Put it into context, use associations, experiment with a variety of memory techniques. In addition, ask questions whenever you have the opportunity to make sure you understand and can make sense of the material.

Questions for Thought

1. What would you guess are the three listening-related factors that most frequently prevent students from paying attention to lectures?
2. Where do you sit in your classes? Who do you sit with? Does either the location of your seat or your relationship with your classmates affect your listening?
3. Do you take notes in class—or in some classes? Why or why not?

Things You Can Do Now

1. Practice two different types of note-taking techniques in one or more of your classes. Which method works best for you? Do you have some classes where taking notes is more helpful than in others? What factors explain this difference?
2. When you are in class, pay attention to the things your instructor does as a communicator. Jot down a list of what your instructors do that helps your listening, and what they do that interferes with your ability to listen well.
3. What class do you find easiest to listen to and remember the material? Why? What subject do you find most challenging in this regard? Identify the class you find least interesting, and list three good reasons why the material may one day be of use to you.
4. Experiment with different memory techniques to see if you can find an effective method of remembering what you hear in class.

8

LISTENING CHALLENGES YOU MIGHT FACE

Everyone confronts a slightly different set of listening challenges. In looking toward the future, however, four situations will have a particularly powerful impact on your listening. If you are well prepared to tackle each of them, you are likely not only to enjoy greater personal satisfaction, but you will also have the potential to make a significant contribution to others.

Listening to Those Who Have Different Cultural Orientations

The world is becoming smaller every minute; the chances that you will interact with someone from another culture nearly every day are increasing. Campuses are becoming more diverse through efforts to expand their student profiles. As you and your friends travel and study abroad, you gain new insights and unique experiences that enrich your understanding of other people and places. The consequence of this situation is that you will be doing more and more listening to those who do not share your values, priorities, or world view. Are you prepared for this challenge?

When listening to those who don't think like you do, it is particularly important to make sure you accurately understand their messages. The skills of comprehension, interpreting, and evaluating will all be extremely useful to you. Not only do you need to consider their background and past experiences when you listen (interpreting), you will also need to withhold judgment and refrain from imposing your personal bias and perspectives on their ideas (evaluating). While difficult, communication will never be effective unless you are able to discern the nonverbal communication and try to empathize—to see the situation from their perspective.

Nonverbal communication is one of the key ingredients for both expressing empathy and accurately interpreting what you hear. Cross-cultural communication, however, provides additional challenges since nonverbal behaviors may have very different meanings in different environments. The amount of eye contact communicators expect and its meaning is one example of how cultural differences can challenge the accurate interpretation of messages. In Asian cultures it is often rude to maintain direct eye contact with those who have a higher status than you. When listening to someone from an Arab culture, however, Americans may find the eye contact so strong that it becomes distracting. While American students are encouraged to interact in the classroom and to question what they hear, young people in other countries may have learned not to challenge their instructor or disagree with what is presented in class.

Even the importance of listening may vary and depend in large measure on a person's background and previous experiences. Whenever you find yourself making judgments about a person's nonverbal behavior, it's useful to determine whether your interpretation needs to be adjusted to recognize cultural dimensions that will enable you to come to a more accurate understanding of the message.

Questions for Thought

1. What are common assumptions Americans make that may inhibit cross-cultural communication effectiveness?
2. Which component of the listening process do you think is most important for effective cross-cultural communication?
3. Have you experienced a cross-cultural misunderstanding? Describe the situation and how it might have been avoided.

Things You Can Do Now

1. If you have friends from another culture, talk with them about their experiences with American speakers. What challenges did

they confront? What communication differences were most apparent to them?
2. Select a culture in which you have a particular interest, and explore the differences that impact communication. What finding was most surprising?
3. What do you think could be done in schools to help everyone better understand and adjust appropriately to cultural differences in communication? Propose at least three initiatives.

Gender and Listening

Although there is disagreement over the origins of gender differences and whether nature or nurture has the most influence on behavior, there is no denying that men and women communicate—and listen—differently.

One of the most obvious gender differences in listening results from the typical differences in men's and women's interests. While most men pay attention to sports and accompanying team and player statistics, women may do better discussing their daily activities and the subsequent feelings generated. Research has shown that women are more relationship-centered than men; they pay more attention to nonverbal communication, are more likely to identify feelings accurately, and are themselves more expressive communicators. Men, on the other hand, generally tell more stories and focus on less personal topics when speaking informally to their friends.

While some gender differences are becoming less distinctive, women still tend to state their opinions and beliefs less forcefully and less directly than their male counterparts. Women tend to pose their ideas as questions rather than as facts. For instance, if you wanted your friend to study with you a woman might say, "What are you doing tonight?" If the person seemed available, the woman would then venture, "Would you like to study together?" A man, on the other hand, is more likely to be direct and say something like, "I've got to study tonight and it would be great if you would join me."

Interestingly, the most definitive distinction between male and female listening has been found to be based in the brain's hemisphere. Brain MRI imaging studies have shown that, when listening to material being read aloud, men tend to process what they're receiving in the left (analytical, objective) side of the brain, whereas women tend to process in their whole brain, tapping into the right (emotional, responsive) side as well as the analytical side.

What does all of this mean for you as a student? If you are on teams or working with both men and women, it is helpful to recognize that differences in perceptions and the subsequent interpretation of messages may be, in part, because men and women simply see the world through different lenses and process through different sides of the brain. If you are prepared for these differences, your interactions and decision-making tasks should go more smoothly.

Questions for Thought

1. Do you agree that men and women listen differently? Describe the experiences that lead you to this conclusion.
2. Do you think the differences in listening are best explained by fundamental biological differences, or are they primarily the result of how boys and girls are raised and socialized? Defend your answer.
3. Would you rather work with a group of all men or all women? Why? What differences would you expect?

Things You Can Do Now

1. Ask your friends to describe how you behave as a listener. Are any of your behaviors strongly gender-linked? Do you agree with their assessment?
2. Become more aware of your own listening style and determine whether any of your behaviors are gender-linked. Do you maintain strong eye contact when talking with both men and women? Do you provide an adequate or an extensive amount of nonverbal feedback when someone speaks to you?
3. Talk with a woman who is working in a predominantly male workplace (like at a construction site or in an auto-mechanic shop) or a man who is working in a predominantly female role (like a nurse or office receptionist). Ask them if they are aware of any differences in their listening behavior compared with others in their work team or department.

Listening with Technology

Staying "connected" with friends has been made easier with advances in technology. Instant messaging, wireless accessibility, and cell phones make communication possible around the clock. The problem is that when you are in class, it is impossible to listen well and continue to communicate through these devices. Such multitasking, which you might think is just the right amount of distraction, prevents you from focusing on the material being presented.

You might feel like you have "spare time" while listening to your instructors talk. You are right—recall that we can process the information we hear much faster than the average speaking rate. However, this bonus time needs to be used to go over the subject of the presentation; using it to focus on an entirely different topic only means that you are less effective in both situations.

As we have discussed, lectures often include PowerPoint slides as part of the presentation. Here again, it is easy to be distracted rather than assisted by the visual component of the message. You will need to exercise self-discipline so that you benefit from the visual elements by deliberately linking them to what you hear. When your goal is to understand what you hear, the process takes up all your time and energy. Listening is a "total involvement" activity—you cannot listen effectively while you are doing anything else.

The rapid advances in technology also have brought with them the need to "listen" over long distances. Numerous studies have been conducted by those interested in learning more about how the listening process changes and what obstacles become more apparent when partners are not communicating face-to-face. Since access to nonverbal communication is limited, the listener's ability to interpret the sender's meaning is limited. Often, too, the style and tone of messages is different when technology is present. Listeners become bored and disinterested without the speaker's knowledge, so there is no opportunity for him or her to further adapt or clarify the message. While tasks might be accomplished, it is nearly impossible to develop the same close relationships characterized by trust and mutual respect when communicators are on the phone, teleconferencing, videoconferencing, or using some other distance technology.

Questions for Thought

1. Do you think that technology changes the way in which communicators behave? What are some specific examples that you have witnessed?
2. What differences do you notice in your listening behavior when you are talking on your cell phone (as opposed to in person)? Do these differences hinder or facilitate your effectiveness?
3. What do you see for the future? Will listening effectiveness continue to be at risk as we communicate more frequently at a distance? What consequences would you anticipate?

Things You Can Do Now

1. Talk with someone who focuses on information technology and ask questions about how he or she views the impact of communication technology on listening effectiveness.
2. Make a list of the ways in which communication technology inhibits listening effectiveness, and the ways in which it enhances effectiveness.
3. What communication technologies are used in your classes? What impact do they have on your learning and your ability to hear, comprehend, interpret, evaluate, and respond to messages?

Listening When Confronted with Ethical Dilemmas

In today's complex world, ethical issues abound. Effective listeners first recognize the ethical implications of what they hear, and then use their skills in interpreting and evaluating messages in order to respond appropriately. They also recognize that friends and classmates from other backgrounds and value systems may view the situation in a different light, and they behave respectfully regardless of these differences.

Get in the habit of asking yourself several key questions when you believe you have encountered a question or problem with ethical implications. Begin with:

1. Who does this decision or situation affect?
2. How are others affected by my decision—is there any potential harm done?
3. What is my role and responsibility?
4. Would I come to the same conclusion if suddenly my decision or behavior became known to everyone in my community?

While the consequences of specific actions are sometimes uncertain, listeners who recognize the ethical dimension of what they hear are in a good position to help ensure that decisions are made in the best interests of all parties involved. Make it a habit to surface ethical implications and bring them out in the open to be discussed. By doing so, you will have taken an important step to ensure that outcomes will be fair and that all those involved will be treated respectfully.

Questions for Thought

1. Do you and your friends regularly consider the ethical implications of your listening?
2. Do you feel you have a responsibility to listen whenever someone wants to talk with you? What if you disagree with them, or believe they are going to do something that won't be in the best interests of others?
3. Do you think it is unethical to "fake attention" as a student in classes? In what other situations are listeners likely to fake attention?

Things You Can Do Now

1. Discuss the ethical issues related to listening with someone from another culture. Perceptions and ethical frameworks differ culturally, and it is interesting to learn how someone else views common issues.
2. Make a list of what you consider to be the five most frequent ethical dilemmas listeners confront.
3. Do you think that your school has a responsibility to surface and discuss ethical concerns in the classroom? Who would you talk with about this subject? What would you say to them?

9

DEVELOP YOUR ACTION PLAN

We have seen, then, that listening is an important part of your daily experience as a student. It is, indeed, a complex process involving skill clusters in receiving, understanding, remembering, interpreting, evaluating, and responding to messages, and takes place in many different contexts. To be a proficient listener and apply these skill clusters appropriately, you will need an action plan that breaks your listening task into three stages—what you do before you listen, as you listen, and after you listen.

Before You Listen

Before you start to listen, you need to prepare by determining or clarifying your listening goal. You may find that you have to negotiate that goal, as necessary, with the speaker so that you'll both be on the same page. Are you going to listen to a friend to provide him or her with therapeutic support? Are you going to listen to a class lecture to gain a better understanding of the material? Are you listening critically to decide if you agree or disagree with a classmate's argument about national security? Do as much background preparation as possible so that you fully understand the speaker as well as the speaker's message. This will enable you to interpret nonverbal communication, situational aspects, past experiences, and other factors as they influence the message.

You will also want to focus on your level of motivation and energy so that you're truly ready to engage in the process. Find important reasons to listen—determine how the information will be useful to you now or in the future, or recognize how much your friend needs your support and encouragement. Listening is a powerful tool and preparing to listen is key to achieving the results you want.

As You Listen

As you engage in the process of listening, your major task will be to keep yourself focused on your job—being the best listener possible. This requires both willingness (recall the LAW of listening from Chapter 5) and considerable self-discipline. You need to recognize when your interest or energy is sagging and do whatever you need to do to get back on track. Perhaps you can shift your position or even have some coffee. You'll also do well to set aside competing stimuli. You may be concerned about getting a flat tire fixed before the weekend, or a quiz you're having in another class. For the moment, put those concerns in a mental "parking lot" and agree with yourself to address these items after you've finished listening.

If you are listening to a lecture, keep your listening comprehension and memory techniques close at hand. Use mental summaries to keep the professor's points stacked up in your memory so you can follow the sequence of the material. Take notes and ask clarifying questions as appropriate and necessary. Above all, take responsibility for your listening success—it's your job and no one else can do it for you.

After You Listen

When you complete your listening experience, review what has just transpired. Summarize the speaker's points to ensure that you've got them. Ask questions or paraphrase back what the speaker has told you so that you know you have it right. Often, you can't recapture the speaker's thoughts at a later time—it's now or never!

When you get a moment, it's also a good idea to review your experience so you can learn and grow as a listener. Did you receive the message clearly? Did you attend carefully? Did you interpret the message correctly? Did you respond appropriately? Your goal is to gradually improve your listening skills so that you can see a difference in your grades and your stress level. Poor listeners not only perform less well as students, they also find themselves constantly worrying about whether they have understood things accurately or if they have missed something entirely.

Questions for Thought

1. Do you prepare to listen differently in different situations and for different speakers?
2. How much energy do you generally spend on listening?
3. Would you say you have a high, moderate, or low level of self-discipline when it comes to school-related responsibilities?
4. Do you agree that listening is complex? Do you anticipate having any difficulty in any step of your action plan?

Things You Can Do Now

1. Practice is always the best way to make sure you will be successful. Write down a list of the things you might do to prepare to listen in one of your classes. Put a check by those that you already do on a regular basis.
2. Imagine that you are about to go for an interview for a summer job. Make a list of background information that would be helpful for you to know in advance.
3. Choose a specific class you are taking, or one that you intend to take. List some specific ways that you can motivate yourself to listen attentively.
4. After listening, it is helpful to review and summarize the speaker's points. What are the obstacles to doing this on a regular basis? What might you do to overcome them?
5. Now that you've come to a greater understanding of what listening is all about and a greater awareness of your own listening behaviors, go through the listening assessment again. How do your responses compare with those at the beginning of this listening journey when you filled out the assessment on page 7 What does this tell you about your abilities as a listener? What are your strengths? What do you still want to work on?

Assess Yourself As a Listener

Many students assume that they are good listeners because it seems to come naturally to them. The best way to really know how you listen, however, is to examine the skills involved in good listening more closely.

Take a look at the following assessment and complete as many of the questions as you can. Be honest—that's the only way you will know what you need to do to improve! After reading *What Every Student Should Know About ... Listening*, go over the questions again and see if you have changed your mind about any of the items. This list should also be helpful to you as you establish and work toward your personal listening goals.

	(4 pts) Not at all like me	(3 pts) A little bit like me	(2 pts) A lot like me	(1 pt) Just like me
1. My friends remember things a lot better than I do.	☐	☐	☐	☐
2. I frequently get distracted or daydream in class.	☐	☐	☐	☐
3. Because I don't think a person's background or past experiences are relevant in communication, I take what someone says at face value.	☐	☐	☐	☐
4. When I argue with a classmate or friend, I focus on winning my point.	☐	☐	☐	☐
5. If I don't know a word someone uses, I figure one word won't really matter anyway.	☐	☐	☐	☐

	(4 pts) Not at all like me	(3 pts) A little bit like me	(2 pts) A lot like me	(1 pt) Just like me
6. In a class situation, there's no point in giving any feedback.	☐	☐	☐	☐
7. If I'm not interested in the subject, I can't make myself listen.	☐	☐	☐	☐
8. I don't worry about remembering things—if it's important, someone will tell me again.	☐	☐	☐	☐
9. If I have expertise, I give friends my advice whether they ask for it or not.	☐	☐	☐	☐
10. I leave it to the speaker to make sure the message is accurate and logical.	☐	☐	☐	☐
11. I find nonverbal communication can be misleading, so I try not to let a speaker's body language distract me from what they are saying.	☐	☐	☐	☐
12. If a lecture is too hard to understand, I just tune out.	☐	☐	☐	☐

6. As you reflect on your listening strengths and weaknesses, create your personal listening plan.

> ## My Listening Plan
>
> Now that you understand what listening is about and have had the opportunity to reflect on your own listening abilities, draw up your own listening plan so that you'll have your own program for self-improvement as a listener. Think of what you can do in each of the six skill clusters: receiving, understanding, interpreting, evaluating, remembering, and responding. (For example: As a listener, I plan to start becoming more aware of my level of attention when I'm listening to a lecture in class.)
>
> 1. **As a listener, I plan to continue:**
>
> 2. **As a listener, I plan to start:**
>
> 3. **As a listener, I plan to stop:**
>
> You will find it helpful periodically to revisit this listening plan to see what progress you've made and to update it with other points as you become aware of them. Improvement as a listener, like any of the communication skills, is a lifelong process. Like exercise and dieting, your engagement in this may vary. But don't give up! Commitment to being a good listener is one of the most productive of all human priorities.

10

WHERE DO YOU GO FROM HERE?

Listening improvement is a journey. Listening is one of the most complex and important things we do as human beings. It's the means by which we connect and stay connected to others. It's the way in which we accomplish the things that are important to us, and coordinate our activities. And, it's the means by which we learn and grow.

Listening is an integral part of your life as a student, and you will find that it will continue to be an integral part of your personal and future professional life as well. Now, while you are a student, is the best time to focus on your listening. Be honest with yourself about your listening strengths and shortcomings so that you can start today to acquire, improve, and practice effective listening skills. These are few things you could do that will have as strong, as long-lasting, and as positive an impact on your future success. Good luck and good listening!